THIS BOOK BELONGS TO ....

AT CHRISTMAS TIME

Published by Peter Haddock Limited,

Bridlington, England ®

Typeset by J&L Composition Ltd, Filey, England.

Printed in Czechoslovakia

Illustrated by Wizard Art, courtesy of Bernard Thornton Associates.

CONTENTS

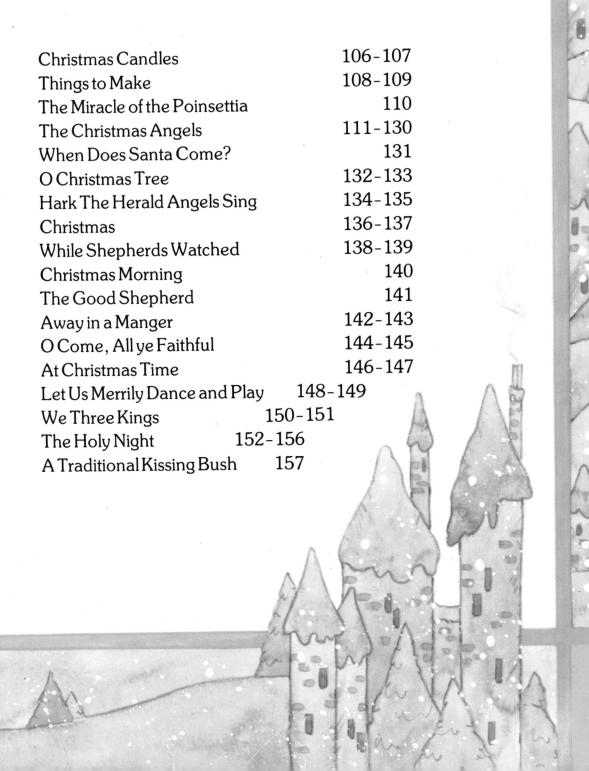

The Little Angel with Silver Hair

The little angel with the silver hair was in trouble. She had been very naughty and now Saint Peter had sent for her. "Come here, naughty one," he said. "You don't seem to understand that everyone here in Heaven has work to do, especially at Christmas time. We all have to make someone on Earth happy." Saint Peter frowned. "But *you* have been lazy and can no longer stay with us. So off you go — you must go down to Earth and make someone happy. Until you do, you can't come back to Heaven."

The very next moment the little angel found herself outside the gates of Heaven. She wondered what to do. So down to Earth she flew and found everything covered in soft white snow. The little angel felt very cold in her thin clothes. The first creature she met was a rabbit who said, "Good afternoon!" The little angel was just about to reply when there was the sound of sleighbells and the patter of hooves. Seconds later, Santa Claus came into view.

When Santa Claus saw the little angel he stopped the sleigh and went over to speak to her. "What are you doing on Earth?" he asked. The angel hung her head with shame and confessed that she had been naughty and lazy in Heaven.

"Lazy, eh?" said Santa. "Then you can come and help me tonight. Hop onto my sleigh!" So saying, Santa tucked the little angel onto the sleigh and off they went. After they had travelled a while, Santa stopped and chose some nice green Christmas trees.

Then he emptied out his sack, which contained Christmas decorations, toys and tinsel. "Would you like to help me to decorate these bare Christmas trees?" asked Santa.

"Oh, yes, I would," replied the little angel with a smile.

"Jolly good," said Santa. "As I'm taller than you, I'll decorate the tops of the trees, and you can decorate their bases."

So Santa and the little angel busied themselves tying the little presents and decorations to the branches of the Christmas trees.

Soon all the toys and tinsel were used up. Santa went off to fetch some bigger presents and promised to collect the little angel on his return. Then the little angel saw that one small tree had no decorations. What could she do? Suddenly she had a marvellous idea! There were gold stars on her dress! She plucked them off and hung them on the branches. What else could she use? Oh! Strands of her beautiful silver hair! These she draped around the tree — and it looked really lovely when she had finished. Even the deer came to admire it!

18

When Santa Claus returned and saw what the little angel had done, he patted her on the head. "That was a very loving thought," he said. "Now we must take all the trees to the nearest village, and perhaps you can find someone who would like to receive your Christmas tree." So Santa and the little angel hopped aboard the sleigh and Santa drove it through the snow until the twinkling lights of the next village could be seen in the distance.

Santa drove the sleigh into the centre of the village and delivered all his Christmas presents there. The angel helped him in every way she could, until at last the time came for her to deliver her own Christmas tree adorned with her beautiful silver hair and gold stars from her dress.

She carried the tree down the path towards a house where three good children lived. The children were helping their mother to wash the dishes as the angel tip-toed into the house and left the lovely tree, together with some gifts.

The angel left the house and flew around to the living room window, then she gazed inside. She saw the children come out of the kitchen and then sing and dance with delight as they saw the Christmas tree. "Isn't it lovely!" they chorused together. "What kind person could have brought it here for us to share?"

The angel smiled with joy and hurried back to join Santa Claus in the empty sleigh.

"Can I give you a lift anywhere?" asked Santa.

"Yes, please," replied the little angel. "Please take me to the wood where you first found me, then I'll fly back to Heaven from there."

"Right," said Santa, shaking the reins of the sleigh. "And thank you very much for all the help you've given me. I'll make sure Saint Peter hears all about it."

"Thank you and goodbye!" cried the little angel as she flew off into the night.

24

When the little angel got back to Heaven, Saint Peter was waiting at the door. "*Now* what have you been doing?" he asked. "Just look at your hair! And where are your gold stars?"

When the little angel told him what had happened to her hair and the gold stars, Saint Peter was very pleased. "Now you can come back into Heaven!" he said.

He was so pleased with the little angel that he gave her some more gold stars and the older angels stitched them onto her robe.

And as for her silver hair ... well, that will grow again!

Oh, Look at the Moon!

You shine on my playthings
And show me their place
And I love to look up
At your pretty bright face.

And there is a star
Close by you; and maybe
That small twinkling star
Is *your* little baby.

Oh look at the moon
She is shining up there
Oh, mother she looks
Like a lamp in the air.

Pretty moon, pretty moon
How you shine on the door
And make it all bright
On my nursery floor.

27

CHRISTMAS EVE

Legend says that, at the first chime of midnight on Christmas Eve, evil spirits temporarily lose their powers and animals are able to speak.

Once Upon a Christmas Time

Lots of snow came falling down
Near a fairy-land town.
It covered everything white,

And the children danced with delight.
Soon they could go out to play
And enjoy the snow in lots of ways.

Like building a snowman three
  metres tall,
Or making a gigantic snowball.
Perhaps going out for a sledge ride,
Or putting on skates and having a
  slide
Across the ice ...
Wouldn't that be nice?

31

While the children were playing
   outside,
Someone in red was taking a sleigh
   ride.
Can you guess who the bearded man
   was?
Of course! It was dear old Santa Claus.

This time he was collecting presents
For very poor girls and boys.
And some kind people had given him
    toys
So that all children everywhere
Could share in the Christmas joys.

One warm hearted snowman
Who lived in a winter garden
Liked to watch the children play.

If he only could have spoken,
He would have wanted to say;
To all children, everywhere,
"Oh do have a lovely Christmas day!"

On Christmas Eve, in a garden shed,
(When children are usually in bed)
Some girls and boys gathered to sing

Christmas carols and songs of praise,
Full of heavenly joy and love.
To God, Jesus and the angels,
High in Heaven above.

And up in that starlit heaven
The angels heard the song.
And the song they heard was so
    wonderful—
That they just had to sing along.

40

"Ding, dong, merrily on high,
In heaven the bells are ringing!
Ding, dong, merrily on high,
In heaven the angels are singing!"

41

Next day back on earth; evening had
    come.
And the children had all gone home
To play with their toys.

And both girls and boys,
Were happy to say:
"Thank you . . . for a lovely Christmas
　　day!"

43

Christmas Crackers

The first Christmas Cracker was invented in the 1840's by Tom Smith, a London sweet shop owner. He originally sold sugared almonds wrapped in paper, containing love mottoes.

He discovered how to make the wrapping go snap when
pulled open. Because of their popularity a factory was opened
to cope with the demand.

CHRISTMAS BAKERY

In Germany and Austria at Christmas time, children help their mothers to bake cakes and biscuits, which they decorate and then use to hang on their Christmas trees.
Some of the biscuits are cut out to the shapes shown on the following pages.

Here is a recipe for:

SPICED BISCUITS

2 eggs
170 g sugar
Pinch ground cloves
Pinch ground cardamom
55 g chopped almonds
42 g chopped candied peel
A little grated lemon rind
55 g ground almonds
1 teasp ground cinnamon
170 g flour

Method: Cream the beaten eggs well with sugar. Add spices and remaining ingredients, stirring in sieved flour last of all.

Roll out thinly, cut into shapes. Bake for 20–25 minutes on a greased baking sheet in moderate oven.

Coat with chocolate or royal icing and coloured sugar. Or pipe with this icing, and decorate with cherries and sweets.

1 egg
60 g icing sugar

Whisk the egg white, then beat in sieved sugar. Beat well together. Put in an icing bag and pipe your design on to the biscuits.

IMPISH BISCUITS

These can be cut out in the shape of imps —
or the Christmas star if you wish.

You will need:

500 g sieved flour
200 g sugar
250 g butter or margarine
Teasp vanilla essence
2 eggs
125 g ground hazelnuts
Filling
some marmalade and icing sugar
mixed together

Method: Cream butter and sugar. Add vanilla
essence and eggs. Slowly add flour and hazelnuts. Mix well. Place on floured board and put
in fridge for 15 minutes. Roll out thinly; cut into
shapes and place on greased tray.

Bake for about 15 minutes in moderate oven.
When cool, sandwich with filling.

VANILLA COOKIES

These are favourite Christmas biscuits. When you smell them cooking your mouth will water! Here is the recipe.

You will need:
200 g flour
150 g butter
50 g sugar
80 g ground almonds
1 teasp vanilla essence
Icing sugar

Method: Place all ingredients on a board and work together to form a dough. Leave for 20 minutes while you grease a baking tray. Roll out thinly and cut into crescent shapes. Bake for 10 minutes in moderate oven. While still warm, dust with icing sugar.

GINGERBREAD MEN

You will need:
115 g margarine
115 g sugar
3 tablesps golden syrup
1 teasp ground ginger
280 g flour
½ teasp bi-carbonate of soda
White and chocolate icing

Method: Warm fat, sugar and syrup slightly and beat till soft. Add flour, ginger and bi-carb and mix until stiff. Roll out thinly and cut out. Bake in moderate oven for 15–20 minutes — cool on wire tray. Using icing, mark in features and buttons. Or you could trace the design on this page and cut it out in cardboard to use as a pattern for your biscuits. Decorate with pieces of glace cherries.

50

COCONUT MACAROONS

You will need:
250 g desiccated coconut
250 g sugar
1 teasp cornflour
5 egg whites
Grated rind of one lemon

Method: Wash the lemon, then grate the rind. Whisk egg whites till very stiff. Add sugar and whisk again till stiff. Then fold in coconut, cornflour and rind. Place in spoonfuls on a flour-dusted baking tray and cook in a slow oven for 20 minutes.

KRACKOLATES

You will need:
30 g margarine
1 level tablsp cocoa
Tablesp golden syrup
Tablesp sugar
7 tablesp Cornflakes (or Rice Krispies)

Method: Melt fat and syrup in pan. Do not boil. Add cocoa. Remove from heat and stir in sugar. Using metal spoon, quickly stir cornflakes until coated. Spoon portions into paper cases. Leave to set.

Angel Fudge

Makes 3 dozen pieces

2 cups sugar	1 tablespoon butter
1 cup chocolate-flavoured syrup	1 teaspoon pure vanilla extract
1 cup milk	¾ cup marshmallow whip

1. Place sugar, syrup and milk in a pan; stir over medium heat until ingredients are well blended.
2. Boil, **without** stirring, until mixture forms a soft ball when dropped into cold water.
3. Remove from heat; add butter, vanilla and marshmallow whip. Do **not** stir.
4. Leave mixture to cool.
5. Beat vigorously until fudge loses gloss. (Fudge will hold shape.)
6. Pour into buttered 8-inch square pan; cut into squares while warm.

The Adventures of Nina the Angel

Once upon a time all the angels in Heaven were getting everything ready for Christmas. They were baking biscuits and cakes. They were making puddings and sweets and wrapping gifts for all the children on Earth. They were all very busy except for the youngest angel who was called Nina. She just got in everyone's way. And to make matters worse she ate the biscuits just as soon as they came out of the oven.

Nina had such a sweet tooth that she couldn't resist trying a piece of cake, and even sweets too. Well — you can guess what happened. Nina got a terrible tummy-ache. She was helping some of the other angels when her tummy-ache got worse and worse. In the end she had to sit down on a little fluffy cloud and hold her poor tummy. Great big tears fell from her eyes. Poor Nina!

She was sitting there looking very sorrowful, with a tiny spot of stardust on her nose, when Saint Nicholas found her and took pity on her. "Well, well, well! What's all this?" he asked in a friendly voice. "You come along with me and I'll give you something for your tummy upset." So saying, Saint Nicholas took Nina by the hand and he led her to a little medicine cupboard in the clouds. Here he gave her a spoonful of soothing medicine ...

Half an hour later, Nina was well enough to go for her music lesson with the other angels. Saint Nicholas was listening to the groups of angels who were singing and playing flutes. Nina joined one of the groups, nearest Saint Nicholas. Soon Saint Nicholas began to hear some funny sounds! He put a hand behind his ear so he could hear better. "Who makes those awful noises?" he asked . . .

Though little Nina was hidden behind the taller angels, Saint Nicholas still found her. "Sorry, Nina," said Saint Nicholas. "I think you'd better not play today. You are making noises as if your flute had tummy-ache. Come back another day and practise."

So poor little Nina, who was feeling rather sad, went and sat on the edge of a cloud and listened to the other angels sing. The music was so soothing that Nina fell asleep . . .

Moments after dropping off to sleep, Nina fell off the edge of the cloud! Before she knew where she was she began falling, falling down to Earth. She was almost down to the ground before she remembered her tiny wings. Fortunately she fluttered them just in time and landed softly in a snowdrift. In the snow covered distance was a little town . . .

Now Nina was very curious about the Earth, and when she saw a bright light from a window, she couldn't resist peeping in. She saw lovely glowing candles on a Christmas tree and a room filled with toys. Just then a little boy called Peter walked into the room. At first he didn't see Nina at the window. He had just picked up his teddy-bear when he saw her. "Gosh!" he thought. "I must be dreaming!"

Peter rubbed his eyes and Nina vanished into thin air! But when he looked at the window pane he saw it was speckled with stardust from Nina's nose.

That evening, Peter's mother and father took him to the Christmas Eve service at church. On the way to the church, Peter saw Nina again and pointed to her joyfully. "Look!" he cried. "It's my angel. And here on the snow is some golden stardust!"

"Yes," said his mother patiently. "But now we must hurry along, otherwise we will be late for church."

So with his mother and father, Peter entered the church. He liked to hear the singing in the church, and after prayers the choir began to sing, 'Silent Night, Holy Night'.

Then Peter heard a really beautiful sound. It was a silvery voice which he could hear above all the others. He looked around in wonder, and there upon a pillar near the ceiling he could see the little angel. It was she who was singing so beautifully. Peter smiled at her happily and Nina smiled back.

71

Late that night Nina travelled back to Heaven. Her little flight to Earth had been very exciting. She had made friends with a boy called Peter, and she had learned what a nice place the Earth could be when everyone sang praises to God. But the greatest thing that Nina discovered was that she had a beautiful singing voice! "Saint Nicholas will be pleased," she smiled. "And tomorrow I'll sing my favourite carol for him ... Silent Night, Holy Night. All is calm, All is bright ..."

CAROLS

From the Greek word 'Chorus' comes 'Carol'. The original meaning was a round song or dance or chorus of joy.

As well as Christmas Carols, which are songs about Jesus, there are Midsummer, Easter, May and even November carols.

Silent Night

1. Silent Night, Holy Night! All is calm, all is bright.

'Round yon virgin, mother and child, Holy infant so tender and mild.

Sleep in heavenly peace, Sleep in heavenly peace.

2. Silent Night, Holy Night!
Shepherds quake at the sight.
Glory streams from heaven afar.
Heavenly hosts sing alleluiah.
Christ, the Saviour is born,
Christ, the Saviour is born.

3. Silent Night, Holy Night!
Son of God, love's pure light
Radiance beams from the Holy face
With the dawn of heavenly grace,
Jesus, Lord at thy birth,
Jesus, Lord at thy birth.

A Coloured Drawing Decoration and Needle Case

To make the coloured decoration simply trace picture on opposite page on to a piece of white or coloured card. Decorate using coloured pencils, cut to shape, then hang on Christmas tree with piece of ribbon. *To make the needle case you will need* 2 pieces of blue felt 11 cm × 11½ cm. 2 or 3 pieces of woollen material. Ribbon for loop 8 cm. Embroidery threads. Needle. Tracing paper. Carbon paper and pencil.

First trace off the design on the next page and using carbon paper transfer the design on to one piece of blue felt. Do the embroidery next, following the stitch diagrams given. Now cut both pieces of felt to the outline shape of the

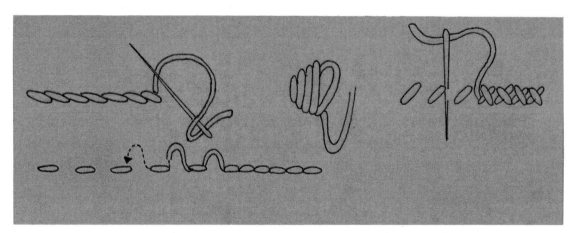

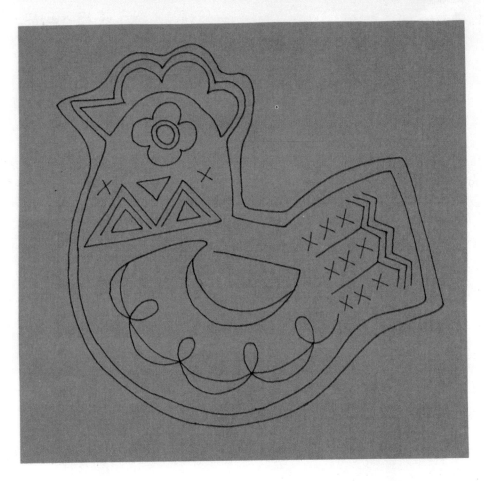

bird, using the transfer pattern. Cut the woollen pieces slightly smaller; tack them between the two pieces of felt, and at the same time catch in the ends of the ribbon loop for hanging. Now neatly stitch through all thicknesses from top of head to tail of bird. Place one or two needles and a few pins inside to finish off this pretty little gift.

A Scented Wardrobe Sachet

Take two pieces of muslin (or other fine material) 13 × 7 cm. With equal sides together, stitch round, leaving a small opening. Turn to open side. Fill bag with dried lavender (from the chemist). Close the opening, trim bag with lace and add a ribbon loop for hanging. Hasn't it a lovely scent?

Gift Wrapping Ideas

A gift looks better if it is wrapped in lovely paper. Here are some ideas to follow to make your gifts look extra special. If you follow the pictures here you will find a way to wrap most presents.

To make a Pretty Trimming

A rosette on a gift always improves it. Using a pretty ribbon or special wrapping tape, fold it over a piece of card the size you want your rosette. Slip off the card and bind the ribbon in the centre. Tie a short piece of ribbon over the binding thread. Follow the pictures. There is your rosette.

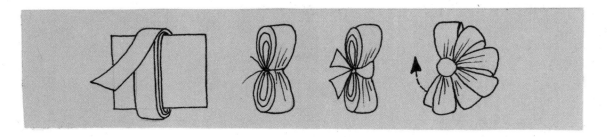

A Hanging Ornament

If you are lucky enough to have a shortbread mould you could make a similar ornament to this. Dust the mould with flour then press it on some rolled out modelling clay. Carefully lift the mould and let the shape dry.
Then paint the embossed parts with poster colours. Glue a ribbon hanger on the back and use as a tree or house ornament.

Making Christmas Decorations

Table Decoration

You will need:
Eight circles of felt in mauve.
Eight round green beads.
Needle and thread.

Thread on the beads and felt as shown in the picture. Tie off the ends of thread, fitting the circle around base of candle. Ask an adult to light the candle for you.

The Snowman

Cover a toilet roll tube (including one end) with white paper as shown. Cut a circle of cardboard 8 cm across. Paint this black and also a 2-cm deep band around the top of the tube. When dry, cut hole in circle of card and pull down over the tube to the edge of black paint. Paint on two eyes and buttons (or cut out in paper and stick on). A red nose and ribbon or paper scarf completes the snowman. If you like you can trim him with a tiny fir branch and toy. He would make a pretty gift for Mummy.

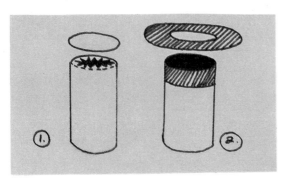

A Walk in a Christmas Wonderland

On Christmas Eve the snow began to fall, and soon it had made everything white. Three children; Sarah, Rebecca and Peter were feeding the squirrels and birds at the bottom of their garden.

Rebecca offered her cake — a doughnut — to one of the birds to peck at. One squirrel suddenly hopped closer to Sarah and spoke: "As you've been so kind to God's hungry creatures, we hope you will be blessed."

A moment later, Peter, Sarah and Rebecca found themselves being given small presents by a kind old lady. All around them the lamplight glowed golden. It was as if the town had become enchanted.

"Don't worry," said Sarah, the oldest child. "The squirrel told me we would all be blessed. Well, perhaps this is our blessing!"

"That's fine by me!" said Peter. "Because I'd like to ride on that rocking-horse over there."

When Peter and the two girls had each had a turn on the rocking-horse, Sarah stopped to look in a shop window. Rebecca and Peter walked on a few metres and came upon a man who was fixing Christmas trees into wooden bases — so that the trees could stand upright in people's rooms.

Rebecca then saw Santa Claus, with his own tiny Christmas tree and a sack beside him. He gave Rebecca a big red balloon and wished her a Happy Christmas.

Meanwhile, Sarah had been gazing into a shop window. There were toys in the window; a teddy-bear, a clown, a donkey and a baby deer. "Which toy would you choose, Peter?" she asked.

"I'd choose the donkey," said Peter.

"Oh, I'd pick the teddy-bear," said Rebecca. "Teddy-bears are so soft and cuddly!"

"Oh I don't know," signed Sarah. "I think I would love the clown — because it would make me smile on a rainy day."

The three children walked on and saw a sweet stall ahead of them. On the counter of the stall were some dolls made out of dried plums, wired together and then dressed in clothes of coloured paper.

Suddenly — much to Rebecca's surprise — four of the dolls began to do a little dance on the side of the counter. "I don't believe my eyes!" she cried. "Did you see that, Peter?"

"Yes," said Peter. "It's just like a Christmas fairy tale!"

Around the other side of the stall, Sarah had been buying her brother and sister some candy. When she saw the candy, Rebecca soon forgot about the dancing dolls.

As they walked on, the children heard the sound of hooves clip-clopping through the snow. From the pavement they watched as an old Christmas-time carriage pulled by two horses came through the centre of the town. "Perhaps it's carrying some parcels for Santa Claus," suggested Peter.

93

Rebecca, Sarah and Peter walked on to a quiet part of the town where an old church stood. Its windows were lit up with a welcoming glow, so the children walked towards it. As they walked closer, Peter suddenly saw a golden star falling down from the sky.

The star stopped, and when the children looked again they saw the baby Jesus in a crib. Peter, Sarah and Rebecca knelt beside the crib and left presents there that the old lady had given them. The baby Jesus smiled . . .

Just then (in the Christmas Workshop Bakery) in Heaven — a little angel was taking some dough-nuts to the cupboard.

Suddenly the little angel knew he had to let the cakes fall down to Earth. A little star had told him so.

The angel flew for a moment, and gently tilted the tray of doughnuts until they began falling — falling down towards the town.

On their Christmas Wonderland walk, Peter, Sarah and Rebecca were nearing home, when suddenly Peter cried out with surprise, "Look! It's raining doughnuts!"

"Gosh!" laughed Sarah. "We can take some home with us. It will save our Mother from doing too much Christmas cooking."

"They taste delicious, too!" said Rebecca. "I've never tasted *anything* like them before. They're ... they're quite *heavenly* to eat."

When the children went indoors, they found the Christmas Tree set up and presents placed neatly around it. "Did you enjoy your walk in the garden?" asked their mother.

"You wouldn't believe it!" said Peter. "We've seen all kinds of wonderful things like talking squirrels, and stars falling from heaven."

"I *would* believe it," answered their mother. "Because I saw a star fall from heaven too! It landed in the garden, and I've hung it at the top of your Christmas tree!"

Christmas Verses

Ring out wild bells.
Ring out with a chime
For everyone,
This Christmas time.
Sing out you angels.
Sing out with a song
For everyone,
This Christmas Eve morn.

Sing Out With a Song!

Hear the music play.
At the close of day.
Watch the new stars shine,
Twinkling in time
To that Heavenly rhyme!

Ring out and sing out!
This special night!
Fill the world with song.
Come on! Sing along!
For this is a night
Like no other one.
This is the night
That Jesus was born!

Raisin Men to Eat

These figures are easy to make if you follow the diagrams below. You will need 12 large seedless raisins and a shelled hazelnut for each figure, a piece of marzipan or cork for a base, and strong fuse wire to make skeleton shape. Following diagrams 1, 2, 3 and 4, mould your basic shape.

A THE SWEEP: has a cardboard ladder, a coil of wire with wool tassel for brush and a top hat made from patterns 1, 2 and 3 on page 103. A sugar pig is tucked under one arm and a tiny piece of cloth is used as a neckerchief. Mark a face with coloured pencils.

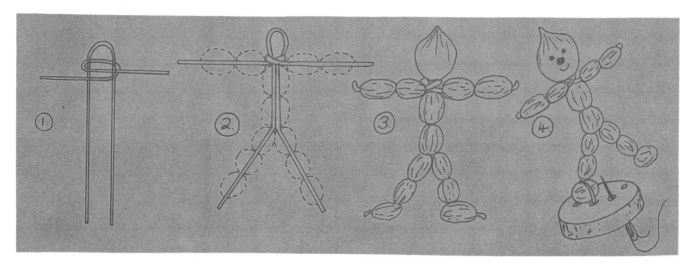

B THE PRESENT BRINGER: is made like the sweep but his body is three dried apricots. Pattern (M) makes his party hat. He has a gift in one hand and a fir branch in the other, a tissue paper scarf and wool strands stuck on for hair.

C A CHRISTMAS REVELLER: He has a top hat like the sweep. His umbrella is made as in diagram (S) on page 103 — with a pipe cleaner centre. A paper collar and tie and cardboard bottle make up his figure.

D THE ZULU: Pattern (K) makes a halo type head-dress, with curls of wool for hair. Tiny strings of beads fit neck, wrists and ankles. The skirt is a circle of tissue slashed and tied round her waist. The sack holds coffee.

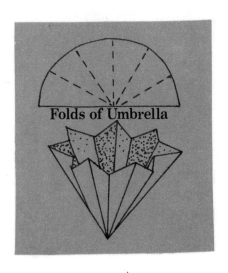

Folds of Umbrella

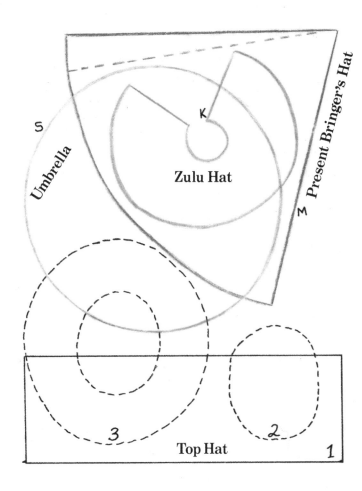

CHRISTMAS PUDDING

A dish made of wheat or corn boiled in milk. Can you imagine it?

This was originally Christmas Pudding as it is known today.

Other ingredients such as eggs, prunes, and meat were added to make it more interesting. When cooked, it was poured into a dish and called 'Plum Porridge.'

Cooks later added more meat and suet which was wrapped up in the scalded intestines of pig or sheep and boiled. Once cooked it could be cut up into slices.

The beginning of Advent is the traditional time for making Christmas Pudding. Every family member must give the pudding a stir and make a secret wish. Stirring from East to West is the proper way to make a Christmas Pudding, honouring the Three Wise Men.

PUDDING

CHRISTMAS CANDLES

In olden times pagans lit fires to the sun. Christians lit candles to the Son of God.

The twelve days of Christmas was a time when the Christmas festival was held. This first happened more than 700 years ago. A candle, specially prepared was lit every night between Christmas Eve and the Eve of 6th January. — Thus the twelve days of Christmas.

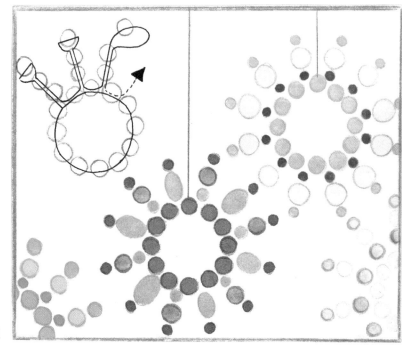

Things to Make

A Tree Ornament

You need 12 beads in each of four sizes. On fuse wire thread 12 round beads. Form into a circle leaving one long end of wire. Thread on three more beads (different sizes) then bring wire down through second and first beads, through next one on circle (see diagram), then wire up three more beads, and so on, until you are back where you started. Twist wire between beads to finish off. Tie on a thread or tinsel loop and hang on tree.

A Fir Cone Figure

You will need: Fir cone. Red card. Piece of red ribbon. Tiny piece of fir branch. Small tree toy. A few very short strands of wool. Slice of cork for base. Cotton wool. Portion of nylon tights. Felt tipped pens. Glue. Stick cone upside down on to cork base. Roll cotton wool into ball and wrap in nylon tights material. Mark features with felt pen or cut out pieces of felt for eyes, mouth, cheeks and nose. Stick head to top of cone, and to this stick strands of wool for hair. A semi-circle of card will make his hat.

Trace off these patterns and cut out of red card. Fold the cloak pattern and stick edges. Make cuts down from top point as in Diagram 1. Stick hazelnut on top. Cut two small circles for eyes from black felt or paper and stick in position. Stick on red oval for nose and 2 circles for cheeks. (see picture). Form the hood pattern into a cone as before. Stick on head. Spread glue round edge of hood and bottom half of nut, and on top of hat. Carefully stick on cotton wool. Fold arm pieces in half and stick into place each side of body. Stick on 2 paper or felt buttons.

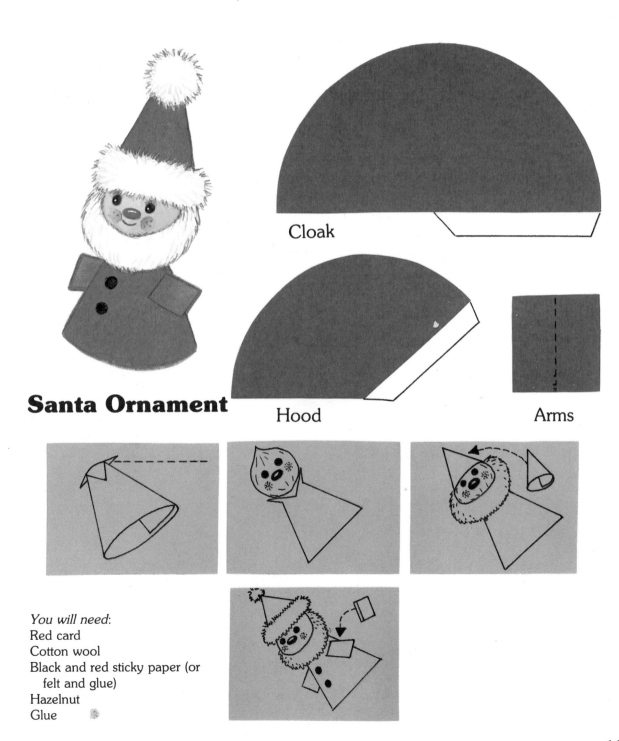

Cloak

Hood

Arms

Santa Ornament

You will need:
Red card
Cotton wool
Black and red sticky paper (or felt and glue)
Hazelnut
Glue

THE MIRACLE OF THE POINSETTIA

An ancient Mexican legend tells of a small peasant girl who wanted to take a gift to Jesus at midnight mass on Christmas Eve. She had no gift to take so angels appeared to her and told her to pick some weeds and take them into the Cathedral.

She entered the Cathedral and was immediately laughed at by everyone inside. Suddenly the top leaves burst into a flame of scarlet. The people fell to their knees while the little girl proudly offered her gift at the crib.

The Mexicans call the Poinsettia 'Flower of the Holy Night'.

The Christmas Angels

"Goodness gracious me!"
  Said the keeper of the Christmas keys.
"Now why should I need to remember
  the 24th of December?
Of course!" he cried. "I do believe
  it is the date of Christmas Eve!
Oh dearie me, oh dear.
I forget it every year!"

"I hope it's not too late
for this very important date!"
Said the man with the Christmas keys;
(after sneezing a Christmas sneeze).
He opened wide a golden door
and out the Christmas angels poured!
They wore dresses of pink and white
and carried presents of colours so bright.
What a wonderfully happy sight
to behold on a Christmas night!
A land of dreams and sheer delight,
full of song — laughter and light.
Each year the angels made toys
(for those very special girls and boys
who did no wrong throughout the year).
And no matter where those children were
the angels would take great care,
to bring them angel-blessed dolls;
or books, or clowns, or cakes or play-balls.
But even better than their angel-toys
Were the *blessings* the angels brought
to those good little girls and boys.

Three good children looked into the night
Watching the snow turn everything white.

114

Their names were Allan, John and Jill.
And out beyond their window-sill
They could see the old steeple
And hear the town people
Singing carols on Christmas Eve.

Tomorrow would be Christmas Day
And the children hoped to play.
Already they had a plan
To build a great snowman
At least a metre tall!

"If the snowman is a friend,"
Said Allan, "He might just send
Our sister Sarah a toy.
And bring her some Christmas joy!"
(Sarah was upstairs sleeping)

"We shouldn't worry about toys,"
Said Jill. "Because some girls and boys
Aren't as lucky as we are.
So let's wish on a star
For the happiness of *all* children!"

"Yes!" said Allan. "You're right.
But look! Did you see that light
Flash across the window?
It was *ever* so bright!
Just like a falling star!"

Now that falling star meant that
Their very own Christmas angel
Had landed in Sarah's room . . .

Sarah was sleeping still
And the angel's light did fill
The room, like a glowing smile.
Then the angel knelt beside the child
And kissed her gently.

Sarah wanted a teddy-bear for Christmas.
And that's just what she got!
The angel laid it by her cot.
It was as soft as fairy snow,
And its golden colour seemed to glow
Like warm sunshine.

The Christmas angel also left a trainset
(For Allan the older boy
Who liked a clockwork toy).
For Jill the angel brought down
A happy and smiling clown
With a bell on its hat
Which went 'Ding Dong!'
And finally, for little John
The angel left the sparkling
Christmas tree.

And so we leave that happy home
And travel through the snow again.

The angels travelled to lots of places
Visiting children of many races.
They flew as fast as starlight
In their heavenly flight.
And all to make children happy.

They were so very, very swift
That they could leave a special gift
With a lucky child, in a twinkling.
And then be gone in the blinking
Of an eye.

Many a child had a big surprise
When they opened their sleepy eyes
On Christmas morning to see,
That the angels had left two, even three
Lovely presents.

Now when one little girl was brought
A new pen, she thought,
She would write to the angels above;
Sending them her fondest love,
And thanking them for her gift.

And as it was the angels who brought the
    pen.
She could use it to write and thank them!
On Christmas day many girls and boys
Could thank the angels for their toys.
And many of them did!

One little girl who loved drawing,
Was given a gift that sent her heart soaring.
It was a big box of coloured pens;
And these she shared with all her friends.
(Which pleased the angels when they heard!)

One little girl was given a paint-box.
While her brother received some bright new socks.
Another boy was given a story-book.
And his sister, an apron in which to cook
Things like scones and angel-cakes.

Of two twin sisters, one got a broom,
With which she could clean up her room.
While her sister was given a tea-set,
Which she thought her best present yet.
So the twins were doubly happy!

Then there was one poor little girl
(With hardly a friend in the world)
Who didn't expect gifts coming her way.
Yet when she arose on Christmas day,
She found a tree and many parcels bright,
Put there secretly on Christmas night —
By those thoughtful little angels!

After the angels' tasks were done,
They began their long journey home;
Where, for a year they would
   work and play,
Until the following Christmas day
When they would fly again to earth.

Now the keeper of the Christmas keys
Was really rather pleased
To be the angels' special friend.
But he wasn't so keen to spend
Any time alone.

So while the angels were away,
He began to sniff and sneeze
And jangle his bunch of golden keys.
Then he thought he heard a knock,
Which gave him an excuse to unlock
The big golden door.

But there were no angels there.
Only clouds and stars and fresh air.
So finally he sat down in his chair.
Star-dust settled on his silver hair . . .
And he fell asleep.

He dreamed; and the song he heard
Was as if sung by a heavenly bird.
Just like his favourite angel's singing.
Then he heard the door bell ringing!
The angels were back!
The keykeeper cried, "Well, hello!
I thought you'd be back hours ago!"
The angels chorused in reply:
"We've been back an hour or two.
But we didn't want to waken you!"

"Oh, I see!" cried the keeper of the keys.
"Right-ho and dearie me!
Well, now it's time for *you* to rest.
So choose the cloud-pillows you like best."
The angels passed through the golden door
Into a magic world that you'd adore:
Skies as royal blue as the seas.
Sweet smelling scents from tall pine trees.

Animals playing in a soft glow
Of heavenly light and cottonwool snow
Birds singing and deer nearby.
And the wind sighing a lullaby.
Rabbits, squirrels and
   star-filled space;
Where everything has its
   natural place.

After making sure things were just right
The keykeeper quietly said, "Goodnight!"
Soon the angels became sleepyheads,
As warm in their fleecy cloud beds
They dreamed the night away.

125

Meanwhile, a million miles away
On earth, it was still Christmas day.
And a lonely orphan boy and girl
Had just returned from a long walk
In the great snow-filled woods.

So just imagine the great joy
Which was felt by that girl and boy
When they found their home aglow with light.
It was shining from a Christmas tree bright.
And there in the middle of the floor
Was a present they'd both hoped for.

It truly was a miracle!
And it wouldn't have been possible
But for the love of a Christmas angel!

Back in heaven once more.
And right outside the golden door.

The keeper of the keys
Had drunk his morning cup of tea.
And he was rather pleased to see
The Christmas angels awake again.
One or two were yawning
Because it was still early morning.
So the keeper of the keys
Whispered very softly: "Please.
What are you going to do today?
Is it to be work — or play?"
"Soon; we'll do some work."
He heard the angels say.
"And then perhaps we'll play.
But *first* we want a song from *you*!"
"Oh me, Oh my! A song from me!"
Cried the keeper of the keys.
"And which song is this?"
"A song from you at Christmas—
For children everywhere!"
Chorused the angel choir.
"A jolly good idea, and I agree!"
Said the keeper of the keys.
"But let's sing it all together.
A one — a two and a three."

129

**WE WISH YOU A MERRY CHRISTMAS
AND A HAPPY NEW YEAR!**

When Does Santa Come?

He comes in the night!
He comes in the night!
He softly and silently comes;

While little brown heads
On pillows of white,
Are dreaming of bugles and drums.

He cuts through the snow
Like a ship through the foam,
While the little white snowflakes swirl.

Who tells him? No one knows!
But he finds the bedside
Of each good boy and girl.

He comes in the night!
He comes in the night!
He softly and silently comes.

While little brown heads
On pillows of white,
Are dreaming of bugles and drums.

O Christmas Tree

1. O Christmas tree, O Christmas tree, Your branches green delight us. O

Christmas tree, O Christmas tree, Your branches green delight us. They're

green when summer days are bright. They're green when winter snow is white. O

Christmas tree, O Christmas tree, Your branches green delight us.

2. O Christmas tree, O Christmas tree,
   You give us so much pleasure.
   O Christmas tree, O Christmas tree,
   You give us so much pleasure.
   How oft at Christmastide the sight
   Of green fir tree gives us delight
   O Christmas tree, O Christmas tree,
   You give us so much pleasure.

3. O Christmas tree, O Christmas tree,
   Your dress will teach me something.
   O Christmas tree, O Christmas tree,
   Your dress will teach me something.
   The hopes and the constancy
   Give power and courage unto me
   O Christmas tree, O Christmas tree,
   Your dress will teach me something.

HARK THE HERALD ANGELS SING

Hark! the herald-angels sing
Glory to the new-born King,
Peace on earth, and mercy mild,
God and sinners reconciled.
Joyful, all ye nations, rise,
Join the triumph of the skies;
With the angelic host proclaim,
'Christ is born in Bethlehem.'
   Hark! the herald-angels sing
   Glory to the new-born King.

Christ, by highest heaven adored,
Christ, the everlasting Lord,
Late in time behold him come,
Offspring of a Virgin's womb.
Veiled in flesh the Godhead see!
Hail, the incarnate Deity!
Pleased as Man with man to dwell,
Jesus, our Emmanuel.
   Hark! the herald-angels sing
   Glory to the new-born King.

Hail, the heaven-born Prince of Peace!
Hail, the Sun of Righteousness!
Light and life to all he brings,
Risen with healing in his wings.
Mild he lays his glory by,
Born that man no more may die,
Born to raise the sons of earth,
Born to give them second birth.
   Hark! the herald-angels sing
   Glory to the new-born King.

CHRISTMAS

The word Christmas means 'Christ's Mass'. A mass is an ancient Christian church service. Christians believe that Jesus Christ was born in a stable about two thousand years ago. They believe He was the Son of God.

Christmas today is celebrated by sending cards and giving presents, lots of good things to eat, crackers, Christmas trees with lights and decorations and fun at pantomimes.

WHILE SHEPHERDS WATCHED

While shepherds watched their flocks by night,
All seated on the ground,
The angel of the Lord came down,
And glory shone around.

'Fear not,' said he (for mighty dread
Had seized their troubled mind);
'Glad tidings of great joy I bring
To you and all mankind.

'To you in David's town this day
Is born of David's line
A Saviour, who is Christ the Lord;
And this shall be the sign:

'The heavenly Babe you there shall find
To human view displayed,
All meanly wrapped in swathing bands,
And in a manger laid.'

Thus spake the seraph; and forthwith
Appeared a shining throng
Of angels praising God, who thus
Addressed their joyful song:

'All glory be to God on high,
And to the earth be peace;
Good will henceforth from heaven to men
Begin and never cease.'

138

Christmas Morning

Christmas morning is a lovely time.
The children's socks all in a line.
Stuffed to the top with exciting things
Like nuts and fruit and a toy on springs.
Crayons and cards, balloons and sweets;
Silver money for children's treats.
Now – off to church some hymns to raise,
To tell of love and joy and praise.

Christmas is about all of these things.
The love and joy the Christchild brings.
He showed us how to love one another
All our friends and sister and brother.
To spread around that grace He brough
As the child the three wise men sought.
Every year on the 25th December –
It is love we really must remember.

The Good Shepherd

The shepherds watched
Their flocks by day,
Making sure their sheep
Did not go astray.
The shepherds watched
Their flocks by night.
And the stars above
All shone so bright.
But one star shone
With God's own Light.

It showed where the
Baby Jesus lay
On a simple manger
Filled with hay.
And to this day
Our Lord is known
As The Good Shepherd.
As we all have heard.
For we are His sheep
Whose lives He keeps.

Away In A Manger

Away in a manger, no crib for a bed,
The little Lord Jesus laid down His sweet head;
The stars in the bright sky looked down where He lay,
The little Lord Jesus asleep in the hay.

2

The cattle are lowing, the baby awakes,
But little Lord Jesus no crying He makes.
I love Thee, Lord Jesus, look down from the sky,
And stay by my cradle till morning is nigh.

3

Be near me, Lord Jesus I ask Thee to stay,
Close by me for ever, and love me, I pray!
Bless all the dear children in Thy tender care,
And fit us for heaven to live with Thee there.

O Come, All Ye Faithful

O come, all ye faithful, Joyful and
   triumphant,
O come ye, O come ye to Bethlehem;
Come and behold Him Born the King of
   Angels;
O come, let us adore Him, O come, let us
   adore Him,
O come, let us adore Him, Christ the Lord.

2

God of....God....Light....of....Light....
Lo! He abhors not the Virgin's womb;
Very....God, Begotten, not created:
O come, let us adore Him, O come, let us
   adore Him,
O come, let us adore Him, Christ the Lord.

3

Sing, choirs of Angels, Sing in exaltation,
Sing, all ye citizens of Heav'n above:
"Glory to God....In....the....highest;"
O come, let us adore Him, O come let us
   adore Him,
O come, let us adore Him, Christ the Lord.

4

Yea, Lord, we greet Thee, Born this happy
   morning;
Jesu, to Thee be....glory given;
Word of the Father, Now in flesh appearing;
O come, let us adore him, O come, let us
   adore Him,
O come, let us adore Him, Christ the Lord.

145

At Christmas Time...

Every year at Christmas time
You can hear the church bells
   chime.

They ring out on Christmas morn;
For that's the day that Jesus was
   born.

And each year from Heaven above
Your own special Angel brings you
   her love.

LET US MERRILY DANCE AND PLAY

1. Let us merrily dance and play:
Santa Claus is on his way
Sing we, sing we, loud and clear,
Christmas Eve will soon be here,
Christmas Eve will soon be here.

2. I'll put out a little dish.
Santa Claus will grant my wish.

3. He will come while I'm asleep,
Dreaming in my slumbers deep.

4. When I wake I'll find a treat.
Lots of lovely things to eat.

5. Let's thank Santa as we should.
Santa Claus is kind and good.

We Three Kings

We three kings of Orient are;
Bearing gifts we traverse afar
Field and fountain, moor and mountain,
Following yonder star.
    O Star of wonder, star of night,
    Star with royal beauty bright,
    Westward leading, still proceeding,
    Guide us to Thy perfect light.

2 Born a King on Bethlehem plain,
  Gold I bring, to crown Him again,
  King for ever, ceasing never,
  Over us all to reign.
    O Star of wonder, star of night,
    Star with royal beauty bright,
    Westward leading, still proceeding,
    Guide us to Thy perfect light.

3 Frankincense to offer have I,
  Incense owns a Deity nigh.
  Prayer and praising, all men raising,
  Worship Him, God most High.
    O Star of wonder, star of night,
    Star with royal beauty bright,
    Westward leading, still proceeding,
    Guide us to Thy perfect light.

4 Myrrh is mine, its bitter perfume,
  Breathes a life of gathering gloom;
  Sorrowing, sighing, bleeding, dying,
  Sealed in the stone-cold tomb.
    O Star of wonder, star of night,
    Star with royal beauty bright,
    Westward leading, still proceeding,
    Guide us to Thy perfect light.

The Holy Night

"Everyone must go to the city of his birth and register his name there!" ordered the Romans.

It was winter and the nights were cold. Joseph and Mary (who was expecting a child) had travelled a long distance and were very tired. They were on their way to the town of Bethlehem where Joseph had been born. Lots of other people were travelling there too to register their names.

The result was that Bethlehem in the City of David became over-crowded that night, and when the exhausted Joseph and Mary arrived at the Judaean town there was no room at the inn. Joseph told Mary to wait while he searched high and low for a room to sleep in; but every single place was taken, every spare room was occupied.

Then the wife of the innkeeper, hearing of Mary's plight, told them of the stable around the corner. It was the part of the inn where the animals were fed, slept and sheltered. So in that stable, in the still of night, amidst the hay and beside the friendly animals, Mary gave birth to a child called Jesus. She

used the wooden manger of the oxen as His first cradle. In the most humble and yet natural of places, Jesus had finally come to the Earth – the greatest gift of God to mankind.

Nearby, in the dead of night, shepherds were on the hills guarding and caring for their flocks of sheep. One of the shepherds noticed a large bright star, more radiant than any other star in the sky. They were all looking up in wonder at this star, which hung like a jewel in the sky over Bethlehem; when suddenly the Angel of God appeared above them. Then, in a blaze of golden light, the holy angel slowly descended. The angel said: "Fear not. For I bring you good tidings of great joy which shall be for all people. For unto you is born this day, in Bethlehem, a Saviour who is Christ the Lord."

At that moment the sky was filled with a heavenly host, praising God and singing, "Glory to God in the highest, and on Earth let there be peace and goodwill towards all men."

The shepherds could hardly believe their eyes and ears. So they hurried into Bethlehem to find the newly born child, just as the angel had said they would. They found the stable directly under that great and glorious star and inside lay Jesus wrapped in swaddling clothes, sleeping in the manger. The shepherds bowed their heads before the baby.

After this they spread news of the angel's visit, and of the heavenly music which came out of the sky. Then they told of the birth of Jesus – who was to become Christ the Lord.

One day in Jerusalem, the jealous King Herod received news that three wise men from the east were searching for Jesus; and were asking everywhere "Where is He that is born King of the Jews? For we have seen His star in the east and have come to worship Him and bear Him gifts."

Herod was troubled to learn of this because he thought of himself as king. So he sent for the wise men, and asked them about the star; and they told him they had followed its guiding light for many days.

Herod sent them to Bethlehem and said "Seek out this child, and when you find Him, come and tell me where I might find Him also."

So the three wise men followed the star which went before them until it came and stood over the stable where the baby lay, but they did not tell Herod where He was. Then they entered the stable and saw the young child with His mother, and they fell down and worshipped Him; and when they had opened their treasures, they presented Him with gifts of gold, and frankincense and myrrh. For they knew that before them lay a baby who was the Son of God.

Every year since that day, this story has been told to children all over the world. Since then, too, it has been the custom to give one another gifts. Just as the three wise men gave gifts to the baby Jesus.

A TRADITIONAL KISSING BUSH

It was believed any girl who was kissed beneath the bush would be sure of good luck and a happy marriage. You can make one very easily:

Just cover two hoops with evergreens and hang mistletoe from the centre, tidy up with red ribbons.